LANKY PAN

By Dave Dutton.

A comic guide to Lancashire sayings by the author of Lanky Spoken Here and Lancashire Laughter and Tears (also all available on Kindle).

See www.davedutton.co.uk

CONTENTS

FOR OPPENERS

Hey up! Long Live Lanky! - from the county that brought you Blackpool Tower; Wigan Pier; L. S. Lowry; the Beatles; Gracie Fields; Eccles Cakes; Coronation Street; Crompton's Mule; Lancashire Cheese; Eric Morecambe; Beecham's Pills; Uncle Joe's Mint Balls; George Formby; Man United; The Grand National; The Co-op; Kathleen Ferrier; Stan Laurel; The Guardian; Frank Randle; Hot Pot, etc., etc., etc.

Nethen!

Have you noticed how the planners are trying to make everywhere look the same; how the EU. daily threatens our way of life in the name of "harmonisation" - providing jobs for a pestilence of bureaucrats; how the breweries have tried to standardise beer down to the lowest common denominator; and - horror of horrors - how you can now get Lancashire cheese in tacky, sweaty little plastic packets?

These are drab days, readers. Unless we do something about it soon, there won't be any point travelling anywhere because every place is going to look exactly the same as anywhere else. Luckily, there is some sort of fightback. Independent breweries flourish. Lancashire cheese comes in all sorts of flavours (Tasty, Crumbly, Creamy)

That's why in an age where the twin steamrollers of bureaucracy and big business attempt to crush humanity into pliant, easily-controlled economic units, a whiff of individuality is like a breath of fresh air in the stale sewers of conformity.

Within our nation are other little nations with their own little idiosyncrasies. Dialect is a stamp of individuality . . . an aural hallmark unique to a particular area . . . a language shaped on the lathe of everyday life and moulded by generations of tongues over centuries of loving use.

My dialect is the Lancashire dialect - "Lanky" - a vibrant, vital, viable and vivid language, full of colour, expressiveness and warmth.

Pessimists have been predicting the death of the dialect "sin Adam were a lad" — yet Lanky is still alive and kicking with both clogs.

Language without dialect would be like fish and chips without salt and vinegar or Eccles cakes without the currants.

Dialect spells home. The farther afield you go, the more diluted it has to become through necessity of communication, for you could not expect "furriners" to understand the subtleties of words like "yedwarch", "thrutch" or "powfagged". (Translation: headache; strain or push; weary or pestered).

And that's partly the reason why I wrote Lanky Panky. You can go into any bookshop in Britain and buy phrasebooks on how to speak French, Spanish, Russian or any language under the sun. In Lancashire, we have a language which to outsiders is as foreign as any of these - and this book tries to explain to the perplexed visitor some of the words he or she is likely to hear on their travels round the county.

It is the companion guide to Lanky Spoken Here! **(now also available as an ebook and hard copy from Amazon)** which aroused a great deal of interest amongst the media and led to a stage show as well as an EMI L.P. with ex-BBC newsreader Robert Dougall as "interpreter".

The books are not intended to be a comprehensive guide to the dialect, but rather an affectionate salute — tongue-in-cheek guides-cum-phrasebooks. Once you start to take a deeper interest in the dialect, you will come to appreciate the ancient pedigree it holds and realise why it has inspired writers down the centuries. As the old poem says:

"There may be a shire 'at is broader,

But there's nobbut one Ceawnty - just one,

At Queen is a Duke on - that's Lanky,

An' there's nowt licks a Lancashire mon."

Sadly, I have seen parts of the Lancashire I love taken away piecemeal: sturdy terraced homes demolished willy-nilly causing the breakup of established communities, with a resultant evaporation of neighbourliness; town centres flattened and unimaginatively homogenised; the coal and cotton industries wrung dry and thrown aside like an old dishcloth; chunks hacked off the county by overpaid bureaucrats who know little of Lancashire and care even less; old pubs demolished or tarted up; Blackpool's Golden Mile denuded of its character; Manchester's Victorian heart ripped out. . . I could go on. But some aspects have gone for the better including smog, outside petties, real poverty - and good riddance, too. Though I do hear that rickets is making a comeback.

Lancashire can and should learn from its past. Lancashire schools should introduce a study of Lancashire literature into their curricula, so that a new generation of Lancastrians may greet again the authors and poets whose work brought so much pleasure in the past: men like Ben Brierley with his Ab o' th'Yate tales, and Edwin Waugh, who was once known as the Lancashire Burns. The teaching of local history would instill some of the civic pride that was taken away by the local government reorganisation fiasco (a mistake which should surely now be reversed).

It cannot be denied that the dialect is nowhere near as strong as it was. Yet with the tenacity of a terrier, it still clings on in pockets of resistance all over the county. Echoes of the Saxons and Norsemen who populated our county still ring down through the ages in place names, accents and expressions.

It does no harm for all us Lancastrians to now and then look to our roots and remember where we came from, regardless of where we are going.

But never mind: **"We've seen Lancashire up and seen Lancashire deawn, Though we know that King Cotton Has lost his gowden creawn. Well we're not beaten yet, And we'll beawnce back, I'll be beawnd, 'Cos we're Lancashire, Lancashire's own!"**

Dave Dutton, Lancashire, 2012. Thanks to Ernest Andrew for the drawings.

See the author's companion guide – Lanky Spoken Here! - on Kindle and other ebooks and visit his website www.davedutton.co.uk

####

A Lancashire greeting.

"Ow arta?"

"Well.Ah'm noan so weel but what Ah met be better and Ah'm noan so bad as what Ah met be wuss"

Chuck thi cap in and come inside!

Starting with…

ALPHABETICAL DISORDER

Forget all they ever taught you at primary school . . it's time to re-learn the alphabet — Lanky style.

When it comes to pronunciation, letters of the Lanky alphabet do not abide by the usual accepted rules of Standard English. They change peculiarly when translated into Lanky. For instance:

A can = E - as in seck (sack) or mek (make) or tek (take). (Art tekkin' it in?)

But, A can also = O - as in 'ond (hand) or sond (sand) or mon (man). Cont understond it?

Ah, but O can also = U - in certain words; eg. a dog is a dug, a man called Tom is Tum and clogs are clugs. (Don't get it wrung).

And what is more, I can end up as E as when string becomes sthreng, light becomes leet and night becomes neet. (Awreet?)

To confuse the matter further, when it comes to the letter H the Lancastrian doesn't use it when he should, and does use it when he shouldn't - as in "Ah wur as 'ungry as an 'orse but Ah've only heaten a hegg with a horange fer hafters". (Hokay so far?)

What is even stranger, the letters D and T acquire H's from nowhere which is enoof ter mek sthrung lurry dhreivurs weep. (Is it dhreivin' yer daft?)

And while we're at it, the Lanky letter R sometimes jumps one place to the left of its own accord as in brast for burst and brunt for burnt. (Is that clear, owd brid?)

And finally, but most importantly, whether it's Christmas or not, the Lanky Alphabet sometimes has "No L" "No L" - as in words like call, fall, wall and ball used as "When Ah heard mi mam caw, Ah fawed off t' waw an' dropped mi baw. .

AN THAT'S AW!

~~~~

PUTDOWNS

If there's one thing a Lancastrian can't abide, it's pomposity.

When in Lancashire, beware - because no matter who you are, whatever high opinion you might hold of yourself or whatever your status in life, the natives have phrases which will cut you down size quicker than a streaker in a sawmill.

How would you like to be on the receiving end any of the following?

Get back int' cheese — there's a maggot short!

(Be off with you, you insignificant little person

Who knitted thy face an' dropped a stitch?

(You're hardly George Clooney, are you?)

Worrart gooin't' do fer a face when King Kong wants his arse back?

(Try going round with a bag over your head.)

Eigh up - peighs've getten their yeds above sticks (Peas above sticks)

These people have got ideas above their station

There's no show wi'out Punch.

(This person likes being the centre of attention)

It's a good job thi balls are in a bag.

(What a shocking memory you have, sir.)

'Er's like Blackpoo' - everybody's been there.

(She is very free with her favours.)

Theaw weren't born - somebody grotched (spat) ont waw (wall) and't sun hatched thi eawt...

(You weren't conceived in the normal way.)

Thi face is lahk me backside - best eawt o' seet

(Your face is like my bottom - it should be well hidden.)

Oi missis - tha favvers a fairy on a muck midden!

(A cry to an overdressed woman.)

Th'art too slow ter catch a cowd. (cold).

(Do hurry up.)

Th'art nowt burra slopstone blonde.

(I see that your hair is bleached. The slopstone is an old-fashioned Lancashire stone sink, whence the insult intimates the colour of the insultee's hair was obtained.)

Thez a face lahk a line o' wet washin'.

(Stop sulking!)

Serves yer right fer playin' Hide-the-Sausage!

(Cry in church to an expectant bride.)

What dust think it is - charity wick? (week).

(You are presuming too much upon my good nature.)

Thaz moor chance o' gerrin' knighted, serry.

(You have little chance of achieving your objectives.)

Anybody who sees thee in t' dayleet 'ull ne'er want run away wi' thee in t' dark.

(You're an ugly devil, aren't you?)

When Ah want monkey, Ah'll poo' t' string.

(Shut up.)

Whose turn is it ter be 'aunted toneet?

(You have a rather dishevelled appearance, madam.)

Ah've seen moor 'air on bacon than thaz geet on thi yed. (head).

(You are going a bit thin on top.)

Tha'd be tall if thi feet weren't turned up so far.

(May I call you Shorty?)

Tha favvers tha's seen thi own arse.

(Do cheer up!)

Owd Mon! Th'art making a noise lahk a Co-op 'orse!

(Sir, your tendency to make loud splashing noises in the lavatory stalls is very off-putting to the other gentlemen using the facilities.)

If Ah rendered thi deawn, Ah wuddn't get enought lard fer t' oil a pair o' spectacle 'inges.

(How painfully thin you are.)

If thi wit were shit, tha'd be constipated.

(You are not as devastatingly funny as you seem to think you are.)

When tha dees, con Ah 'ave bone eawt thi nose fer a coathanger?

(When you expire, your prominent nose bone would handy in my wardrobe.)

When Ah want thy opinion, Ah'll pull t' chain.

(Keep your nose out of my business.)

Yon mon's too numb to know he is numb.

(He is so unintelligent, he hasn't the intellectual capacity to comprehend how unintelligent he really is. A Catch 22 situation.)

If brains were a disease, tha'd be plump-i'-fettle.

(You're no mastermind, are you?)

Ah've seen better yeds on a pint of ale

(What a dim so and so you are.)

Th'art not fowest mon Ah've ever seen, but tha favvers 'im...

(Granted, you are not the ugliest fellow I have encountered, but you look like him.)

~~~~

ROAD SIGNS

Motorists beware! Here are some of the road signs peculiar to Lancashire. Very peculiar.

You are now entering Manchester –
please open umbrella.

Southern Jessies beware – strong
Northern beer (brewer's droop zone).

Stop!

Fly over.

Pennine Road to Bradford – beware
sacred cows.

All Southerners must be accompanied
by their mums.

Gents, please refrain from leaving
lavvy board up.

Motorists – beware motor-cyclists on
black peas.

Beware – ferrets on heat.

Look out for pedestrians with rickets.

~~~~

ALLTERGETHERAGEN!

Lancashire words are like fish and chips - they go together. Sometimes, a whole sentence can be telescoped to form one word bearing no resemblance to spoken English.

Try getting your laughing tackle round these....

Sawreetferthee.

(It is all right for you.)

Erzfawnwityedintpo.

(She has tripped and landed with her head in the chamber-pot.)

Eezertizont.

(He has injured his hand.)

Yonzeez.

(That belongs to him.)

Erzurzawlowerer.

(She is in dire need of a depilatory cream.)

Geeuzakisswilta?

(Would you give me a kiss?)

Astbrowtitwithi?

(Have you brought it with you?)

Izziterzerizziteez?

(Does it belong to her or does it belong to him?)

Eeeyafflaff.

(You have to laugh, don't you?)

Azzertannerpuss?

(Has she taken her purse?)

Izyedzawshapes.

(He has a lumpy cranium.)

Avaddabuttifermitay.

(I have had a sandwich for tea.)

Astastaskastaskter?

(I shall have to ask - have you asked her?)

Interfow?

(Isn't she ugly?)

Ahlsithitmornmornermornneet.

(I will either see you tomorrow morning or tomorrow night.)

Fotchiteerserry.

(Please bring it here, sir)

Corpcartkektoeranthorstukboggarts!

(The fourwheeled vehicle belonging to the Co-operative Society has overturned and the horse bolted off in fright!)

~~~~

THE SECRET SHIBBOLETHS

No matter how good a foreigner (ie. a shandy-drinking Southern Jessie) becomes at aping the Lanky lingo, there are certain words which will always catch him out and brand him or her an outsider. These are the secret shibboleths: "shibboleth" being the word that the Ephraimites could not say correctly when challenged to do so by their enemies the Gileadites.

If you wish to perfect your pronunciation of Lanky sufficiently to mingle unnoticed among Lancastrians take special note of the following:

- **A garage is not a gar-ahj - it is a garridge.**
- **Mauve is never mohve but mawve.**
- **A bus is not a bass but a buzz.**
- **A piece of nougat is not a piece of noo-gar but a piece of nuggit.**
- **Envelopes are not onvelopes but envelopes.**
- **A room is not a rum.**
- **Awmonds are olmonds.**
- **A scone is not a scohne - it's a sconn.**
- **A tortoise is definitely not a tortus — it is a toytoise.**
- **And, of course, dinner is at teatime.**

So be warned.

Ignore these pronunciations at your peril. And if you don't know what happened to the Ephraimites, see Judges XII.

~~~~

LANCASHIRE ANATOMY LESSON

This was Leonardo Da Vinci's original illustration. (He was originally from Oswaldtwistle).

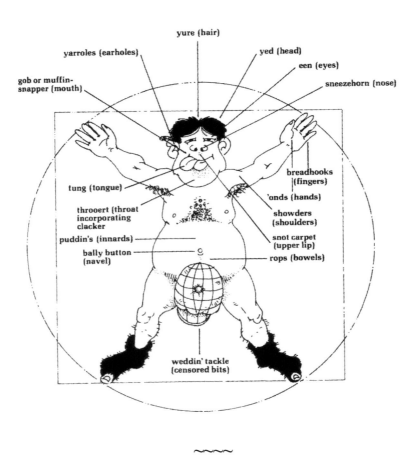

~~~~

"PHILOSOPHY"

Lancashire folk have a great deal of commonsense: the fact that they live in Lancashire proves that. Thus the visitor will often encounter some homespun philosophy proffered by some Wigan Socrates or Ramsbottom's answer to Plato.

If you do not understand the deep fundamental truths the philosopher is trying to convey, don't worry. The chances are that neither does he...

Ponder the following:

A meawse what's nobbut one 'ole's soon takken.

(A mouse with only one hole to run to is soon caught and one should always have more than one avenue of escape in any situation.)

The minutes tha plays thi, tha'll ne'er 'aft work.

(The moments of time you have had off work have gone and you will never have to work them.)

'Ard work never killed anybody but it's made 'em some bloody funny shapes.

(The second sentence indicates some reluctance to believe in the truth of the first.)

Them az az will 'ave.

(Fortune usually smiles on those who don't need it)

A creakin' door'll 'ang a good while on its 'inges.

(Invalids usually have long lives while those looking after them usually die first)

All is not gold that glitters — an' all is not shit that smells.

(Don't be fooled by appearances - of *any* shape.)

Tha doesn't look at mantelpiece when th'art pokin't fire

(You don't have to look at an ugly girl's face when you're enjoying yourself with her.)

A bee in a cow-turd thinks himsel a King.

(An upstart-deflater.)

Ah con do owt except wheel misel in a barrow.

(There are limits to one's capabilities.)

One tale's good till another's towd. (told).

(A one-sided story always sounds plausible - until you hear the other side. Witness party political broadcasts.)

A fool con ask moor questions in five minutes than a wise mon con answer in a month.

Them as beighs (buy) beef beighs bones,

Them as beighs land beighs stones,

Them as beighs eggs beighs shells,

But them as beighs good ale beighs nowt else!

(Perhaps that's why we like our ale so much in Lancashire.)

~~~~

LOOK OUT! IT'S THE LANKY CHAUVINIST PIG!

Question: What is a Lancashire lad?

Answer: *"The genuine Lancashire lad is a being worthy of study. His deep sense of humour; his patient endurance of adversity; his lifelong struggle with want; his indomitable perseverance; his love of home - all point him out as one of a remarkable race. And despite his sometimes rough exterior and uncouth language, your real Lancashire lad is one of nature's gentlemen at heart."* So wrote William E. A. Axon in his book Folk Song and Folk Speech of Lancashire many years ago.

What he definitely wasn't talking about was that heartstopping horror the Lanky Chauvinist Pig.

Here is some help in identifying him. . . though if you ever meet an LCP, you won't need any clues - you'll *know*...

The Lanky Chauvinist Pig has an IQ of 27 with his flat cap on - and 12.5 with it off. The LCP is one of the species that Darwin missed. He is a quaint anachronism, a throwback to the Dark Ages, a slight hiccup in Mother Nature's grand scheme of things. In other words, he's a right pillock.

He is a man of few needs. Observe, the Lancashire Handkerchief - or the Lanky Hanky...

Which he uses, thus –

19

Moral: **Never** shake hands with a Lanky Chauvinist Pig...

To preserve his manhood in the eyes of other LCPs, he would never be seen dead carrying any of the following in his hand:

(a) A bunch of flowers; (b) a gill (half-pint) glass of ale; (c) an umbrella; (d) a poetry book; (e) his wife's coat. To be seen by cronies carrying any of these would qualify him instantly as a Mary Ann.

LCP wives never nag their husbands in bed. If they are tempted to do so, retribution is swift as the LCP practices his own method of administering an anaesthetic by forcing his wife's head under the sheets and breaking wind. Thus ensuring a good night's sleep (for him if not his wife).

The LCP has a unique and infallible way of slimming. When he staggers home from the pub, he picks up his dinner and throws it at the wall thus in one stroke cutting down his calories and saving on washing-up liquid. (Some LCP wives inured to this dinner-slinging have become adept at eating the meal with a knife and fork as it's sliding down the wallpaper).

The LCP always has a warm welcome for Yorkshire folk — he sets fire to their trouser-legs.

He has scrupulous standards of hygiene - he always insists on spraying his whippets with DDT before allowing them in bed with him and the wife.

The LCP is very possessive. To ensure nobody touches his beer when he goes to the pub lavatory, he places his false teeth in his pint. (This is also a standard gambit for acquiring the ale of unsuspecting southern jessies.)

When walking through the park or grassland, the LCP always allows his wife to precede him by three paces. This ensures that whatever's lurking on the ground, his wife stands in it first — whereupon he executes a nifty sidestep.

The LCP thinks that a rank outsider is a southern jessie with BO. But he'll always oblige him with exhibition of clogdancing - usually on top of his head.

~~~~

THE YORKSHIRE COAT OF ARMS

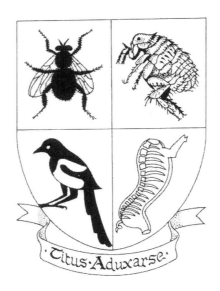

As most people know, Yorkshire is a little place just outside Lancashire. A Yorkshireman is merely a failed Lancastrian and his emblem is a red rose suffering from anaemia. At Rugby League matches, the Yorkshire contingent yells at the Lancashire crowd: "Lancashire Hot Pots!" To which the Lancashire spectators respond with "Yorkshire Puddings!" They never learn.

Here is the official Yorkshire coat of arms, as found on the walls of Payfersod Hall, just outside Heckmondwike.

As you can see, this contains a fly, a flea, a magpie and a side of bacon...

Reasons for this are obvious. A fly will sup with anybody - and so will a Yorkshireman. A flea will bite anybody - and so will a Yorkshireman. A magpie will chatter with anybody - and so will a Yorkshireman. And a side of bacon is never any good until it's been hanged...(finish it off yourselves).

~~~~

USEFUL ABUSEFUL PHRASES

It's as well to know when you are being insulted in Lancashire. Though usually extremely hospitable, the native Lancastrian can become aggressive when he considers you have offended his honour - such as by knocking over his pint pot or driving over his favourite pet whippet.

Here are some of the things he may say to you. (NB. Using any of the following to a fair-sized Lancastrian is a quick way of finding out at first-hand the quality of hospital food in the county.)

Dust want a leather 'n' timber kiss?

(How do you fancy a kick from my clog?)

Ah'll tek a bit o' thi wom (home) in me pocket.

(There'll be bits of you missing when I've finished!)

Thaz a face lahk a constipated bloodhound!

(Smile, please.)

If tha'd hafe a brain, tha'd be an ape.

(You are somewhat deficient in grey matter.)

Th'art purrin' (putting) thi yed in a dog kennel!

 (Don't mess about with me or you'll get in trouble.)

Tha favvers tha's bin punched gether.

(You look slightly deformed.)

Tha skens (squints) enoof ter crack a lookin'-glass.

Tha skens enoof ter upset an 'orse an' cart.

Tha skens lahk a basket o' whelks.

(Remarks to one with cross-eyes. There was a famous pub in Tyldesley called Skennin' Bob's, named after a crossed eyed landlord)

Ah'll gi thi some clog toe pie.

(Not an invitation to dinner - this is an offer to give you a good kicking.)

Thaz a nose lahk a blind cobbler's thumb!

(Your nose is a funny shape!)

Th'art nor 'avvin' *me* on a butty.

(Don't try it on with me.)

Ah'll snatch thi breath!

(I'll kill you!)

Ah'll tek it eawt thi ribs!

(Pay what you owe me or I'll have the satisfaction of giving you a good hiding!)

Art tawkin' ter me or chewin' a brick?

(You are conversing rather indistinctly.)

Ast getten a feather up thi arse?

(Remark to one laughing over-excessively.)

Dust wanna faceful o' dandruff?

(This refers to a butt in the face. In Lanky, a butt is also known as a tup - also the name colloquially given to a ram because of its habit of butting. Thus, the town of Ramsbottom is known locally as Tup's Arse.)

Ah'll lamp thi yerrole!

(I will hit you in the ear!)

Th'art too fow t' make arse'oles on - warty uns.

(You are too ugly to make anuses out of - not even work-day ones. "Warty" has nothing to do with warts - it means workday: as in "warty clothes" (workday clothes) as opposed to Sunday best. Thus the insult infers that the person referred to is not even fit material for fashioning the most inferior kind of anus - a double insult!)

Tha makes me bum wink.

(I am fed up with you.)

I hope thi balls turn square an' fester at corners.

(A fate too terrible to dwell upon.)

If thi brains were made o' gunpowder, there wouldn't be enough ter part thi' 'air.

(You're obviously an idiot.J

Who rattled t'side o' *thy* hutch?

(When I want your advice, I'll ask for it...)

Ah wouldn't wash thy underpants fer £1 a rub.

(You are breaking wind somewhat excessively.)

'E's so mean that when he gets up of a mornin', 'e looks under' t bed fert see if 'e's lost any sleep.

(He's an old Scrooge.)

~~~~

EXCLAMATIONS!!!

Nay belike!

(Surely you jest?)

Shittot!

(Great!)

Fairation!

(Let us have some fair play please)

Guwomwithibother!

(I do not believe you)

Partly wot!

(Nearly. Not half!)

Four cakes!

(An exasperated euphemism)

Clap 'owd!

(Hold Tight)

Nethen!

(Depending on the tone, it can means hello, beware or now for something different)

Gulladowdlad!

(Well done, sir!)

That lick's cock-feight!

(Superb!)

Weigh!

(Stop!)

It'll come to ye!

(You'll get paid back)

Think on!

(Remember)

Winkayltum!

(We have defeated them)

Bidooin'!

(Hurry)

By the stars!

(Good heavens!)

Gi o'er!

(Stop that at once!)

Owd Mon!

(For goodness sake!)

Shape thisel!

(Get your act together)

What con yer do when yer clogs let watter in?

(An exclamation of resignation)

Ah cawn't speyk!

(I stand amazed!)

~~~~

FAMILY MATTERS

Here is some healthy advice to outsiders who a tempted to meddle with family matters in Lancashire. ***DON'T.***

Here are some phrases to keep in the family

They're lahk tribe uv Israel.

(They are a rather large family.)

Kick one - an' they aw faw deawn. (all fall down).

(They are very close-knit.)

We're related to 'em - their cat ran through our backyard.

(We are not all that closely related really.)

They fun eawt (found out) what wur causin' it.

(They are now taking precautions against having any more children.)

'Eez nobburra lad awom.

(He might be a big shot at the office, but at home he's a cipher.)

'Eez 'is feyther shitten.

(He is a perfect facsimile of his father.)

Nay - 'e favvers 'is mam.

(I disagree — he looks more like his mother.)

They 'ad a bite ut th' apple afore they bowt tree.

(They enjoyed very close relations before they married.)

It's nobbut cowd porridge waarmed up.

(Cold porridge warmed up - a renewal of old love as when a divorced couple re-marry.)

'Eez babbed 'er an' theyn 'a t' get wed.

(He has made her pregnant and they have had to marry.)

'Er'll clog again.

(She will marry again.) (of a widow).

They're livin' o'er t'brush.

They're livin' tally.

(They are cohabiting unmarried.)

'Eez gettent feet undert th' essole wi' t'widder next door.

(He seems to be getting on rather well with his widow neighbour.)

~~~~

T'WAHF

In Lancashire, the men prefer not to refer directly to their wives . . . especially in front of pub cronies or workmates.

Instead, they will call them "t'dragon" opposed to "th' owd dragon" for the mother-in-law) …"t' bride" (if they are feeling charitable) . . . "Our Maude" (even if that's not her name!); th'owd stockin' mender or even "th' owd 'andbrake" when their wives have put a stop to their social activities.

If the husband goes out in direct disobedience of wife's wishes, this can lead to **"a bad wom"** (getting a bad home - ie. being in disfavour at home) or even **"deaf'n'dumb meals'** - prolonged silences at the dining table for an indefinite period. Sometimes also described as **"telly's on but there's no sound"**.

This tactic is an effective method of coercing the husband to abide by his wife's demands: at least until the next time he decides to please himself what he does.

This course of action usually results in the husband **"getting his tap stopped",** forcing him to lead a celibate existence until he repents.

It's a matriarchal society anyway: the strongest characters in Coronation Street have all been women.

~~~~

THE WICK, THE DEAD AND THE POORLY SICK
WI' A SHAWL ON

In a Lancashire household, whenever the local newspaper pLops on the mat, the first page that is generally turned to is the one containing the obituary column.

The latest gossip about "whooz deed?" and "whooz on 'iz road eawt?" (ie. About to die) provides great fuel for discussion among the local community.

Here then are some "dead good" phrases to make you faint' bi wick (glad to be alive)...

Tha favvers thaz bin dug up.

(You have the pallor of a corpse.)

Ah'm only walkin' abeawt fer t' save buryin'-brass 'cos Ah cawn't afford dee.

(The only reason I'm alive is that I am so poor I can't afford the money to be interred.)

Ah'm proper poorly sick wi' a shawl on.

(I'm really ill.)

'Eez dropped off perch. 'Eez popped 'is clogs. 'Eez cocked 'is toes. Gone dee-erd.

(He is now the deceased.)

If 'eez tan (taken) aw 'is brass wi' 'im, it'll aw bi melted bi neaw.

(You can bet he hasn't gone to heaven.)

'E never 'ad a doctor - 'e deed 'uv 'imseif.

(He died naturally - he didn't need a doctor's help to do so.)

Wudta be as sharp in mi grave?

(A sarcastic remark to a person who takes over someone's place on a seat very quickly.)

Cheer up - there's awlus cut.

(A cheerful encouragement to commit suicide in a canal)

Th'art too awkert dee.

(You are too obstinate to expire.)

Simithry.

(Cemetery.)

T' Divil's 'ad porridge and t' Lord's nobbut getten pon fert scrape.

(Said of a deathbed repentance when someone has led a sinful existence. . . ie The Devil's had all the porridge and God's only got the pan to scrape.)

Tha looks pot.

(You look out of sorts.)

'Eez getten a wooden top-cooert. (top-coat).

(He is in a coffin.)

Tha'll never live ter scratch a grey yed!

(You won't live long enough to collect your pension!)

Th'art awluvva wacker.

Th'art wackerin' lahk a tripe doll.

(You are trembling a great deal.)

Never - till Ah'm lyin' on mi back between two pieces o'wood wi' mi gob full o' sond (sand)!

(A Lanky version of *"Over my dead body!"*)

'Ee'd bi wuss (worse) if owt ailed 'im.

(There isn't a thing wrong with him.)

'Ast played a wrong domino?

(Said to someone with a broken leg, this alludes to the proliferation of cheats at dominoes. When a "bad" domino is played by their partners, they give them a hefty kick under the table to draw attention to their mistake.)

And some Lanky remedies.

- **To rid yourself of earwarch (earache): spit in your ear.**

- **To rid yourself of a pimple: rub saliva on it.**

- **To banish a wart: tie a horse's hair round it or sell it for sixpence.**

- **To cure yedwarch (headache): dip a rag in vinegar and water and wrap round head.**

- **To ward off rheumatism: keep a nutmeg in your pocket.**

- **To alleviate swollen glands: boil a potato in its skin, place it in a sock and wrap the sock round your neck.**

- **A facetious "cure" for constipation: shove an umbrella up and bring it down open!**

~~~

WHO'S NOT WHO

Here are some strange-sounding Lanky names which refer not, as the traveller may think, to actual people – but to things…

JINNY GREENTEETH

A mythical boggart based on the green slime seen in brooks and streams, supposed to drag down unsuspecting children to their doom as in "Jinny Greenteeth's gonna get thi".

WET NELLY

A type of cake

MARY ANN

An effeminate man

SWAGGERING DICK

A type of toffee

DOLLY TUB

A large tub previously used for washing clothes

DOLLY BLUE

An agent used for whitening clothes

BILLY WINK

A nursery name for a make-believe man who shuts children's eyes at bedtime. Thus, going to sleep is "getting some Billy Wink.

HARRY LONGLEGS

The crane fly

PEGGY WEGGIES

A child's name for teeth

RICK RACKS

A pair of bones used as a percussion imnstrument

SOPHIE

A sofa

GREEN GILBERT

A "bogey" as in nose detritus

~~~

SOME QUAINT LANKY CUSTOMS

Spittin' on't fire: a great source of amusement especially to old men in taprooms who compete to see who can put the fire out first. It makes a hell of a mess of gas fires though.

Dad's night out: traditionally a Friday…and a Saturday…and a Sunday afternoon….and a…etc

Purrint kettle on: Lancashire folk are always putting the kettle on. It helps if you have a flat head.

Noggin' a stockin': the practice of hiding the hole in the heel of a worn stocking underneath the foot by means of tugging at the toe end and tucking it under. It is very effective with woollen socks but stretches your suspenders to breaking point if you're wearing a pair of nylons.

Bottomin' th' eawse: bottoming the house. This means giving the house a thorough cleaning from top to bottom - not walking about without trousers.

Donkey-stonin' t' steps: whitening the doorstep and the surrounding flags by rubbing them with a "donkey stone". This practice is steadily going into a decline due to shortage of donkey stones caused by the intervention of the RSPCA on behalf of the donkeys. Only joking - it's a sort of pumice.)

Chukkin' t' cap in: a method of ascertaining whether or not one is welcome in a house by opening the door and throwing one's cap in. If it stays inside it either means you are welcome; there's nobody in; or your cap has landed on the fire.

Standing a round int' pub: the Lanky mon always insists on standing a round in the pub. In fact he'll stand around all day and let you pay for the ale!

Fancyin' pigeons: a disgusting habit carrying a penalty of six months for the first offence.

Cryin' a notchel: announcing in the paper that a spouse won't be responsible for the other's debts.

~~

SOME SOUTHERN MISCONCEPTIONS ABOUT LANCASHIRE

Let's put the record straight.

"It always rains in Manchester."

Wrong. This is a filthy falsehood put about by a Southerner who, on a visit to Manchester, caught a trout in his turnups in Albert Square and was arrested for illegal fishing by a policeman with a bill and webbed feet.

"They spend fifty per cent of their time in the pub." Wrong. This is a gross slur. The figure is nearer ninety per cent...

"They absolutely hate Southern people." Wrong. We absolutely love Southerners - fried in batter, with a few chips

"They do nothing but race their whippets all day long." Wrong. We used to race whippets but we stopped doing it because they kept beating us.

'They eat their young and paint their faces blue." Wrong. The blue faces are a manifestation of the extremities of the cold climate - and we only eat our young when there's an R in the month.

"Of course, my dear, they never ever bath". Wrong. We bath extremely regularly - once a year when we go to the seaside. How do you think *Black*pool got its name?

"All Lancastrians wear clogs and shawls and flat hats all the time" Wrong. We only wear them in bed.

"They constantly live on a diet of tripe." Wrong. The only time we see tripe is when Southern football teams come to play us up North.

"And of course they are totally illiterate"

Bolax!

~~~~

DESCRIPTIONS

Lanky has some biting phrases to describe people's attributes and characteristics. I sincerely hope you don't find yourself on the sharp end of any of these.

'Er could talk under-watter.

'Er could meither a nest o' rats.

'Er could talk fer Lankysher.

'Er's getten a tongue lahk a length o' tripe.

(She's a talkative woman.)

'Es plaitin' 'is legs.

(He is somewhat drunk.)

'Is heels 'ave getten master uv 'is yed

(Yes, he is definitely drunk.)

'Is nose cost as much brass fer t' paint as a row o' good- size heawses...

(He suffers from a boozer's cherry nose.)

'E wouldn't gi' a frog a jump.

'E wouldn't gi' a lavvy door a bang.

'E were born wi' cramp in 'is fist.

'E wouldn't part wi' t' smook off 'is porridge.

(He is an extremely mean man.)

'E's bowlegged wi' brass.

(He is rather well-to-do.)

'E's norra full shillin'...

'E's no oil in 'is lamp...

'E's not geet aw 'is cheers awom. (his chairs at home).

(He would make a good Prime Minister.)

'E's aw theer wi' 'is mint drops.

(He knows what's what.)

'Er's moor edge abeawt 'er than a butcher's saw.

(She's nothing but a show-off.)

She'd bend deawn to a bulldog.

(She is a little oversexed.)

'E'd pee through somebody's letterbox, then knock ont door to ask heaw far it went.

(He is a cheeky man.)

'E lahks smell of 'is own trumps.

(What a vain man he is!)

'E's etten moor than 'e gradely should.

(He hasn't left any food for anyone else,)

'E's getten no 'inge in 'is back.

(He is not a creep.)

'E's a face lahk a ruptured custard.

(He is not a pretty sight.)

'Er's poxed up ter t' eyebrows.

(She is suffering from a social disease.)

'E favvers a Red Indian.

(He looks hot and bothered.)

Ah'v a bum like a cherry/lahk a blood orange.

(I was on the curry last night.)

They'n moor twists than a game o' pontoon.

(They are a very devious lot.)

He's got ten bob on 'imself...

(He holds himself in inordinately high regard.)

Th'art as much use as a balloon bowt skin.

(You are totally ineffectual.)

'Er's a face lahk a well-slapped arse.

(She has a somewhat ruddy complexion.)

'Ers getten footbaw eyes – one at 'ome and one away

(She suffers from a pronounced squint)

'E's a gob lahk a parish oven.

(He is very fond of the sound of his own voice.)

Tha favvers tha's fawed off a flittin'. (flitting = a house removal).

(You are an unsightly mess.)

'E wur three feet between 'is eyes!

(He was a rather large individual.)

There's moor (more) work in a glass of Andrews.

(He's one of those social security scroungers.)

Thi willy must be full o' spud-wayter. (potato water).

(I fear you could be infertile.)

'Er has a face lahk a bulldog lickin' piss off a thistle

(She has a somewhat dour countenance.)

If Ah'd a face like thine, Ah'd teach mi arse ter speak.

(God, but you're ugly!)

~~~~

THINGS WE SAY.

- Being glittering jewels of folk-wisdom that have been passed down along the ages, like mumps, scarlet fever and athlete's foot...

A shut meawth (mouth) keeps flies eawt.

(If you keep your mouth closed, you won't get in bother; so keep quiet and don't repeat others' gossip.)

Second 'un sits on t' best knee.

(The second wife of a marriage frequently gets treated better than the first one.)

'Im int neet wi't rag arm.

(Him in the night with the amputated arm - a nonsense retort for parrying inquisitive people who want to know who you are talking about.)

Muck midden pride - a carriage weddin' an' a wheelbarrow flittin'.

(The price you pay for being "showy".)

Beauty's only skin deep - but it's a bugger when tha 'ast use a pick ter ger at it...

(There's ugliness and then there's *ugliness*.)

Tha met bi born but th'art not dee-erd yet.

(You might be born but you're not dead yet, ie. you might be congratulating yourself that you are doing very nicely - but a lot of nasty things could happen to you before you die, so don't be too sure of yourself.)

Stopped fer bobbins.

(Out of work - or a temporary hiatus.)

Smile and t'world smiles wi' thi — cry an' tha'll pee less.

(Basic Lancastrian philosophy.)

Tha con caw mi what tha wants, but don't caw mi late fer mi dinner.

(Insults are one thing, a proper sense of priorities another.)

Ah've no moor use fer it than a duck 'as fer an umbrella.

(I haven't any use for it whatsoever.)

It's a poor arse that can't rejoice... Better eawt than in...

There's mony a one in t' simithry (cemetery) us'd be fain t' do that...

(Responses to comments of disapproval after someone has "broken wind".)

Tha wants aw thi own road an' a bag purrit in.

(You are spoiled.)

'Arken' t' kettle cawint pon brunt arse.

(Listen to the kettle calling the pan black.)

Tha wants know tale and't tale's master.

(You want to know the lot.)

Ah bet there's moor snotty noses than standin' pricks this weather...

(The cold snap shows no sign of abating.)

Ah've got booath feet in one clog.

(I just can't seem to get started today.)

~~~~

YANKY GOES LANKY

The buck stops here, me owd sugar butty! Far too many people these days talk like they've just stepped out of a cheap American B-movie. Battered into submissive acceptance by a plethora of television imports from the U.S.A. (and I don't mean the Uther Side of Accrington), we are swapping our mother tongue for an uncle tongue - Uncle Sam's to be precise.

It's got to stop. To help reverse the flow, here are some typical "yankifications" I have translated into good owd Lanky...

YANKY: Lay some skin on me...

LANKY: Pass the black puddin's.

YANKY: Keep on trucking.

LANKY: Don't give up your job at Pickfords.

YANKY: Right on.

LANKY: No foreplay ía typical Lanky Chauvinist Pig tactic).

YANKY: Rip-offs.

LANKY: Petty rolls (toilet paper).

YANKY: Hang loose.

LANKY: A bad case of Brewer's Droop.

YANKY: She's far out, man.

LANKY: 'Er's expectin' a babby.

YANKY: She's a real little mover.

LANKY: 'Er's always flittin'.

YANKY: Laid back.

LANKY: The fate of the recipient of a Wiggin butty. (a smack in the gob).

YANKY: He's an acid freak.

LANKY: He likes lots of vinegar on his tripe.

YANKY: A real cool chick.

LANKY: A deep-frozen turkey.

YANKY: Black is beautiful, man.

LANKY: Gi'me a black puddin' ony day, serry.

YANKY: Stay cool.

LANKY: Don't pay yer gas bill.

YANKY: Cop out.

LANKY: In Lancashire, Cop out? (catch) is traditionally asked of anglers after a day's fishing.

YANKY: What's your bag, man?

LANKY: What does the mother-in-law do for a living?

YANKY: Awesome!

LANKY: Fair to middlin'

~~~~

SOME ADVICE

And now a few words of "friendly" advice . . . tek heed or else...

Save thi breath fer t' cool thi porridge.

Let thi meight (meat) stop thi meawth.

(Eat up and shut up.)

Throw thi muck wheer thi love lies.

(Take your litter home with you.)

Tak no notice on 'em - they talk as they worm.

(They converse through their bottoms.)

Don't pull t' pictures deawn - wur not flittin'.

(Father, do stop picking your nose!)

Shut thi' legs — there's a draught!

(Please keep your knees together, madam.)

Don't wait o' shoon (shoes) till clogs wain't come.

(Advice to a young woman who wants to marry "above" herself but might find herself left on the shelf.)

Keep it dark - it met (might) be a black puddin'.

(Nonsense phrase to emphasize that something you have been told, or found out, is in the strictest confidence.)

Spit it eawt — it met (might) spell it.

(Advice to a stutterer.)

Lap up.

(Wrap up warm - it's cold outside.)

Ball off an' bounce.

(Shove off!)

Keep thi' motty eawt, serry.

(Do not meddle in my affairs.)

~~~~

THE GREAT MOGGY CONTROVERSY

1. Take one taproomful of mixed Lancastrians.

2. Add beer.

3. "Stir it" by shouting: "What's a moggy?"

4. Stand back and watch the mixture simmer. The result will be a red-hot potato.. . and if all that seems a bit cockeyed, let me explain:

There is one word in Lancashire of nobbut five letters which at its mere mention has the power to set brother Lanky against brother Lanky and start a civil war throughout the county.

It is the one thing which has more power to divide the county than a whole cartload of planners and bureaucrats put together.

The word is (don't shout it!)

MOGGY!

You see, part of the county says a moggy is a cat. . . part says it is most definitely a mouse! And some even go so far as to say it's also creepy-crawly insects and nits.

In the companion volume to this book - Lanky Spoken Here! - I defined a moggy as being a mouse or tiny insect. That really put the cat among the moggies or the moggy among the pigeons (depending on which side of the moggy fence your sympathies lie).

Moggy battle standards were raised all round the county, resulting in strong letters to the press; hour- long phone-ins with the late Alec Greenhalgh (pro-cat) on Radio Manchester; a running battle in the Manchester Evening News between myself and writer Andrew Grimes; moggy cartoons in the papers; plus shoals of letters and learned scholars of the dialect joining in the general scrum.

The outcome of all which was this: It was agreed that in some parts of Lancashire -mainly the coalmining areas - a moggy is a mouse and in some parts it's a cat (though coming from the part of Lancashire where a moggy is a mouse, I know what it really is....)

So, if you want to start off a good old Lancashire barney, simply casually enquire: "What is a moggy. . . ?" Then run like hell.

Some Moggy Expressions

Moonleet Moggy. (moonlight moggy) - a beautifully descriptive term for a loose woman. . . one who stays out late at night.

Moggy is also a nickname for a very small person.

Moggy muck - mouse droppings.

Moggy meight (mouse food) - cheese.

Moggy off! Lanky for "Go away!"

A Moggy-er or Moggy-catcher is a cat (but only in those parts of Lancashire where a moggy is a mouse).

Moggy-yed - an abusive call after someone with nits in their head.

Moggy Pie - is, believe it or not, a pie made out of baked mice and used as a cure for bedwetting.

~~~~

GOING, GOING GONE…

It is a sad thing when a good word dies. Here are some apt and colourful Lanky words which although dead or dying, seem much more expressive than their tame modern counterparts. Perhaps we could give them the kiss of life?

Yonderley – an almost poetic adjective meaning absent-minded or not quite with it.

Hiddlance – in secret.

Rift – belch.

Aliker – Vinegar.

Powler – to ramble about, drinking.

Scarrick – a tiny piece of something.

Good lorjus days – Good Lord Jesus, what days.

Addle – earn.

Gobslotch – glutton.

Warch – ache.

Ninny 'ommer – Fool.

Day skrike – daybreak.

Arsey versey – head over heels.

Jannock – honest.

Edge o' dark – Twilight.

~~~~

AN OLD LANCASHIRE TOAST.

Meyt (food) when we're hungry

Drink when we're dry,

Brass when we're short on it

An' Heaven when we die!

~~~~

BITS'N'BOBS

(some useful words and phrases to help you on your way)

It wur a reet knacker-wratcher.

(It was rather hard work.)

Babby-werk. (baby-work)

(A childish action by a grown-up.)

Parish lantern.

(The full moon.)

Parish candles.

(Stars.)

Axum back.

(Ask them back.)

Beggar uv it wur...

(The irony of it was...)

A stonkin' greight lorronem.

(A great many of them.)

Mangy.

(Ill-tempered.)

Mi eyes're swoppin' corners.

(I am growing extremely tired.)

Pisspoor.

(Very poor. A criticism, not a financial statement.)

Mitherin'.

(Pestering, annoying.)

Witchert.

(Wet-shod: the state of having wet feet.)

It's aw baws (all balls).

(A reference to the game of snooker.)

Spon-new, or Sponny.

(Brand-new.)

Neet ullert.

(Night owl - used to describe person who stays out late at night.)

Incense.

(Not the stuff they use in churches and Thai massage parlours. In Lancashire, "I couldn't incense him", means "I couldn't make him understand".)

Lugg.

(A knot in the hair.)

Bacon tree.

(Pig.)

Cryin' a notchel.

(Giving public notice - was usually in local paper - that one party won't be responsible for debts of another: usually a spouse)

Car thi deawn.

(Please sit down.)

Showin' yer monkey.

(Acting up or becoming bad-tempered.)

Th'oon.

(The oven.)

Cow clap.

(Cow pat.)

Sindin' t'clooas.

(Rinsing clothes.)

If Ah cawn't catch thi mi dog will!

(Said when throwing an object at someone you are pursuing.)

Pissfartin'.

(Of little consequence.)

Hanch.

(To snap at - as a dog snapping with its teeth. The Hallowe'en game of biting at apples on strings is known as hanch-apple.)

Nast.

Dirt. Filth. Or as used by a workman before changing into clean clothes — "I'm in me nast".)

Obstrockolus.

(One of my favourites. A frequently-used Lancashire mispronunciation of obstreporous.)

Rammy.

(Food that smells off.)

Thrashers.

(Old slippers still in use.)

Rider-eawt.

(A brewery representative calling at pubs.)

Stotherin' drunk.

(Staggering drunk.)

Yorkshire Oyster.

(An egg.)

Peighlin' away.

(Hurrying. Also used of a sexual encounter as in "Ah wur peighlin' away when her husband walked in".)

Bant.

(String.)

Wi' leet on um.

(We came across them.)

Buzzert.

(Moth.)

Darkin'.

(To go spying on courting couples at night.)

Arrin' an'jarrin'.

(Arguing)

A ponful.

(A lot.)

Th'art a maulin' scone!

(You are a meddlesome so-and-so.)

Ah cud do wi' a dose o' brokken bottles.

(I'm constipated.)

Parrotin' on. Pappin' on.

(Talking excessively.)

Sooly.

(Dirty.)

Deggin' can.

(Watering can.)

Back eend.

(Autumn.)

Thrayklin' worn. (Treading home).

(To wend one's way home.)

Ah cud eight (eat) a scabby-yedded Chinamon.

Ah cud eight neb off me cap.

(I am extremely hungry.)

Cut.

(Canal.)

Tha shapes lahk a wooden 'orse.

(You are useless.)

Britches-arse steam.

(Very hard manual effort.)

Cheese'n'Tripe!

(A blasphemous euphemism.)

Tek thi face a-rattin'!

(Advice to ugly man...)

~~~~

FUNNYOSSITIES

You can expect to have the mickey taken out of you in Lancashire. Watch out for the following...

Traveller: Excuse me, I wonder...

Lanky Mon: (interrupting) Tha'd wonder wuss (worse) if t' crows built in thi yed and took thi nose fer a nest egg...

Or, (Slightly stronger version):

Lanky Mon: Tha'd wonder wuss if t' crows built up thi arse - tha'd wonder how they'd getten sticks across!

Traveller: Excuse me - have you got the correct time?

Lanky Woman: Aye - a quarter past mi garter an' hawf-road (halfway) up me leg.

Traveller: (bemused) Thanks very much.

A: I've just been thinking...

B: Oh aye - Ah wondered what that rattle were...

Child: Mam - Ah've nowt sit on...

Mam: Well shove thi thumb up thi arse and sit on thi' elbow...

Beware of this following prank which can only be used on New Year's Eve.

A: Where are you going?

B: Ah'm gooin't' look fer t' mon who 'as as many noses on 'is face as there are days in t' year.

After which person A is expecting to see a man with 365 noses on his face until it suddenly dawns on him that there's only one day left in the year. Ho Ho.

The traveller should also be wary when he sees a sign saying "For the blind", with a collecting box underneath it outside a grocer's shop.It has been known for the grocer to wait until the box is full - then go out and buy himself a new blind for the shop-window.

Lanky Mon: Hey thee - what's a turd weigh?

Foolish Traveller: I haven't the faintest idea...

Lanky Mon: (hardly able to contain his glee) "Ere's Ten Pence - go an' weigh thiself"

If the traveller is wearing a cap, he should beware of the following prank...

Lanky Mon: Hey Ah say - let me see if there's a wee in thi cap....

And when the unwary traveller passes him the cap in all good faith, the Lanky mon whizzes it gleefully across the street shouting: "Wheeeee!"

A: I see (local fishmonger) has just been fined £50.

B: What for?

A: For showing his cod in t' shop winder.

(A play on the word 'cod" which could either mean the fish of that name, or what a codpiece covers.)

Picture a tiny man on a large horse in a parade...

Heckler: Oi - shortarse . .. why dussn't geroff and ger inside it?

Small Man: If its arse were as big as thy gob, I'd 'ave no trouble at all.

Traveller: But I thought...

Lanky Wit: Tha knows what thowt did - he followed a muck cart and thowt he were followin' a weddin'. Or, — he shittibed an' thowt he were on t' petty.

Cry to someone scratching their head... "Turn 'em over an' gi't' young 'uns a chance!" (meaning give the young nits a chance to come on top.)

Person rushing up: Ah've come fer t' tell thi Ah can't come - an' if Ah come Ah can't stop...!

If in Lancashire you buy a meat and potato pie and there is more potato than meat, the bits of meat are whimsically called sheawters (shouters) because they are so far apart in the pie that they have to shout to one another in order to converse. Also known as a Hurray Pie - because every time you find a piece of meat you shout Hurray!"

"Go an' see if yer outside - and if yer return while yer away, I'll keep yer 'ere till yer get back . .

(Even Einstein couldn't even work that one out.)

Irate Housewife: Beauty is only skin deep....

Husband: Then tha must've bin born insahd eawt.

~~~~

Printed in Great Britain
by Amazon